THE RESPONSIBLE PARTY

(Revised Edition)

by

RICHARD L FREITAG,

Citizen

Bloomington, IN  Milton Keynes, UK

AuthorHouse™
1663 Liberty Drive, Suite 200
Bloomington, IN 47403
www.authorhouse.com
Phone: 1-800-839-8640

AuthorHouse™ UK Ltd.
500 Avebury Boulevard
Central Milton Keynes, MK9 2BE
www.authorhouse.co.uk
Phone: 08001974150

First published by AuthorHouse 4/25/2007

ISBN: 1-4184-3296-2 (sc)

Library of Congress Control Number: 2004093330

*Printed in the United States of America
Bloomington, Indiana*

This book is printed on acid-free paper.

<u>Warning!</u>

Readers, your attention please. Understand that you are reading a small book which is a *call to action* for those citizens who are not happy with the actions, activities, policies, politics and platforms of either of the two existing major political parties. The purpose of this work is to create a new and innovative approach to American politics – in essence, to form a foundation of thoughts and ideas upon which to build *a new, a third, major political party.*

The plan envisioned and the action called for will appeal to those who believe that the only way to effect any positive political change is to restructure the basic framework of the political arena within our United States of America.

This *new, major and permanent political party* will represent the interests of those who presently feel they have no voice in their government. The intent is not to create more rhetoric (we already have enough of that), but rather to act with deliberate intention for the good of our nation and its citizens through the policies, programs and actions of a new, third major political party.

Table of Contents

Preface

The ideas expressed in this little book began to take shape well over a decade ago. Writing down the concepts being offered here for your consideration began as a way of venting my frustrations with the current political systematization of our uniquely American system of government. However, over time, I have taken this a step or two beyond my original intention. That is, rather than merely venting and being critical, complaining about what I feel are the shortcomings and problems within systematized politics and systematized government, I am offering ideas and thoughts – a vision for a brighter day and a better way. I do this because

I have always believed that simply being critical really takes very little, if any, creative thinking or vision. Pure criticism, in my view, is nothing more than observation and fault finding. Critics abound, and many seem more concerned with projecting an aura of intellectual superiority than with actually changing anything.

So maybe it's time for something different. What if critics would apply just some of their vast wisdom, their massive intellectual capacity, to offering up options to fix the faults they find and the problems they observe? What if critics could become more pro-active, rather than simply dwelling in the pool of negativity they seem to enjoy creating? I would certainly have a great deal more respect for what they have to say under these conditions. Fault finding, complaining and whining affect little change.

So you see, I'm just not all that impressed with critics.

With that said, I decided that if it was indeed my desire to create positive change within the political arena and thereby make positive change possible within our systematized government, I would need to offer up possible alternatives to the "business as usual" presently found in the two party system of government. Not wanting to be merely another critic, I have offered up alternatives and a variety of possible solutions for your consideration.

The original manuscript for this work was reviewed by a number of friends and even a relative or two. Heartfelt thanks to David Haake, John Wallace, Chris Weilep, Henry Radandt, Don Miller, Charlie Mueller, John Baker, Mike Solberg and my wife Kathryn. All offered up suggestions for improvements, enhancements and corrections to the thoughts and ideas expressed in my first attempt. I am most grateful for their suggested revisions, clarifications and support in general.

One of my friends, in particular, deserves special mention in terms of making this book a reality. John Lowe sat down with me and read aloud the entire manuscript. As he did this, I made notes. During this process, corrections and additions necessary to clarify the intent of the ideas became very clear, and I feel the "flow" of the book was improved a great deal.

Generally, authors dedicate their work to their spouses and families, thanking them for their patience and understanding during the writing process. My wife, Kathryn, has been all of that and more.

But I would rather dedicate this little book to those American citizens who, like me, believe that the time has come to put an end to the flagrant corruption found within systematized government, which is perpetuated by the two party system (with emphasis on *system)*. These are the citizens who believe that the changes in politics and government we envision cannot and will not be made by the membership of either of the existing two major political parties. These citizens, to whom I dedicate this book, have had enough of the two party system and the elected officials who give precedence to the interests of those two parties, while the primary interests of citizens are relegated to secondary consideration at best, and at worst to a mere afterthought.

So, this book is dedicated to you, my fellow political dissidents.

Richard L. Freitag

Eau Claire, Wisconsin

I. Introduction

One spring evening in the early 1990s, I was watching a
nationally broadcast news program when the news anchor
shared a brief piece concerning a recent government study.
Initially, the content of this report seemed less than noteworthy. However, contained in this brief news blurb was
an underlying, unreported message – a statement concerning both a political and socioeconomic undercurrent
within our nation. And despite the fact that more than a
decade has passed since that evening, this message has
remained fixed in my mind. The particular government
study reported on that evening made it glaringly obvious,
to me at least, that a third major political party is needed

This brief and seemingly bland statistical study done by some governmental bureaucracy about the financial makeup of our American Society at that time went something like this: ***According to a recent government survey, 15% of the U. S. population lives below the poverty line as defined by $15,000 or less of annual household income. The report further went on to say that 14% of the U. S. population lives above the wealth line as defined by $75,000 or greater annual household income.***

The news anchor then moved on to the next news item of the day.

I could not.

It was impossible to move past that story because I was transfixed, not by what I had just heard, but rather, by the unmentioned implications of the figures cited in the study.

Introduction

Overwhelmed by the unspoken message contained in this tiny news brief, my thought process was, and has remained, focused on the political polarities implicit in that report. That government survey and the findings reported therein have given me cause to consider at great length what was being said about the political, social and economic makeup of our society, as well as how the various segments of our society are, or are not, represented politically.

Consider this: there exists a basic belief as to which major political party supposedly represents the interests of the 15% of the population living below the poverty line. This is, at least, the claim of that party, and many seem to believe it. There also exists a commonly held belief about which major political party represents the interests of the 14% of the population living above the wealth line. Again, this political position seems to be generally accepted as true.

The question, then, that will not go away, is this: ***Which of the two major political parties represents the interests of the 71% of the population of this nation who are neither wealthy nor impoverished but who pay for the excesses of those on either end of the financial spectrum of American society?*** While both major political parties claim to represent the interests of the 71% majority, there remains the hard truth that the 71% known as the middle class, while funding government expenditures which benefit both the very rich and the poor, are doing so without a political voice to represent their interests. The very poor can't pay, and the very wealthy feel it should be up to someone other than themselves to pay.

Both of the major parties pander to the interests of the 71% during all political campaigns and prior to every election only because it is necessary to their purpose of fund raising. Make no mistake about this: ***their only goal is to raise money***. Do not believe for a moment that either of the two major political parties have any particular interest in the well being of middle class America. In their view, we exist to be exploited politically and financially, our pockets pilfered in the interest of providing funds for those members of society in either the upper 14% or the lower 15% of our nation's economy, while nothing whatsoever is done for, to, with or about the middle class.

Certainly, concerned citizens in a democracy should be members of political parties. Without citizen involvement, how can there be a "government of the people?"

Have you struggled to find justification for membership in either of the two major parties? Do you feel that either of the major parties is a good political "fit" for you? Given the politics and policies of either of the major political parties, do you find yourself interested in membership in either? Do either of the major parties speak to your needs or represent your interests or your point of view? Really? Have you tried to convince yourself that one or the other major political parties speaks for you and those like you?

Little evidence exists to support the conviction that America's middle class has any sort of real political representation. The fact is, neither major political party represents the interests of the 71%.

Both major political parties have polarized themselves. They either represent the interests of the very wealthy or the very poor - the extreme liberal or the extreme conservative. In either case, this polarization is nothing more than a matter of a fictitious identity which results in political impasse, gridlock and a stalemated legislative process. This political polarization – this "either/or" representation of one or the other end of the socioeconomic spectrum – leaves those of us in the middle class without representation.

Was it not written somewhere that "all are created equal" — not just the very wealthy or the very poor, but *all* American citizens?

Given the political posturing of the two existing major political parties and their radical "left wing" or "right wing" political positions, those of us who believe that both positions are equally silly and unreasonable, even stupid, are left to flounder politically and fall into a representational chasm. While both parties claim to be the champions of the 71%, the truth is that neither is, nor do they care. We 71%ers deserve to be represented just as much as the 29%. But don't expect to see that representational void filled by candidates of either of the major political parties in the near or even distant future given the political polarization of each party.

So, just in case you haven't gotten it by now, I'll go back to the question: **Which of the two major political parties speaks on behalf of the interests of Americans who are neither rich nor poor?**

In truth, neither!

The Presidential Election of 1992 especially, and even the one following in 1996, though to a lesser degree, demonstrated plainly that there are citizens in this nation who are not pleased with the political antics of our government and/or the political platforms and positions of either of the major political parties. Mr. H. Ross Perot's 19% popular vote in the 1992 election shows us that nearly 1 in 5 voters cast their ballots for Mr. Perot in a futile attempt to send a message to our elected officials in Washington. Among other things, the message expressed an unwillingness to go on tolerating the hypocrisy of the legislature's actions (or inactions). Arrogant disregard, even contempt, for the political interests of middle class Americans by elected representatives (who we are constantly reassuring us that they have our best interests in mind) will no longer be tolerated.

Many of us who voted for Mr. Perot back in 1992 are proud of the ballot we cast for him. We voted for Mr. Perot because we wanted to, tried to, felt a need to send an urgent "wake up call" to Washington.

That wake up call, evidently, went unheard.

So, what to do?

Those of us who are not happy with the politics of either major party can continue to complain, gripe, and whine as we listen to the pandering of major party politicians prior to elections. We can continue to get lost in the smoke screen thrown up by the blame game politics practiced by both parties. If we believe what they say, we will continue down the ridiculous path of our past, and nothing will change for us or our nation politically. We will continue to be paid lip service by those politicians who supposedly represent our best interests. The lip service and pandering will affect no change for us whatsoever.

Only proactive involvement can and will affect the positive political change we seek.

Entrenched government systems will not and cannot change until or unless new ground is broken. There must be a new vision, a new philosophy, a new position, a new posture, a new initiative. In short, a new major political party needs to be formed whose elected officials will *truly listen to and represent all of the citizens of this nation, including those of us in the 71% majority.*

The time to take that action is now! The time to form a new permanent major political party is now!

Introduction

Those of us wishing to affect positive political change in the United States of America need to understand that time is of the essence! Political change of the kind we envision can only be affected by organizing, activating and energizing a third major political party. This party will not be about just another flash-in-the-pan, one-shot, independent run at the presidency.

The goal is to form a third major party which will become and remain active on the American political scene until, like the two existing major political parties, it too loses its vision and direction or, more importantly, loses touch with the citizens it is supposed to represent.

II. Fundamental Observations

For your consideration: a review of some of the good and the less than good within our government and the arena of our existing two major political party system.

Good Stuff

It is essential that all citizens of these United States of America, whether happy or not with the present state of politics in this country, recognize that our constitutional republic form of government, implemented with democratic principles, is the best possible form of government in the world. Although it is all too often claimed to be so, our government is *NOT* **a democracy,** but rather, our form of government is a constitutional republic which is defined as a government of **law.** If our system of government was indeed a democracy, we would be subjected to the will of the majority since this idea is the basis of true democracy. Rule by the majority is not the case in our nation. We must understand that although there is certainly citizen participation in our form of government (making ours a form of democracy), we are not a pure democracy. Nevertheless, our system of government is time tested and results in the greatest possible good for the greatest number of citizens. Above all, we must all accept that although our system of government is not by any means perfect, there exists no better model by which to govern a nation in the world today.

If, indeed, this constitutional republic is the finest form of government, and a citizen involvement (democracy) is the best way to achieve this "government of the people, by the people and for the people," which results in the greatest possible good for the maximum number of citizens, what could give cause for dissent? Who would want to find fault with our system of government given that this nation is the longest lasting type of "government of the people" in the world today? Why complain?

Dissent gives rise to change! Our Constitution guarantees all citizens of the United States of America the right to dissent. Dissent is anti-apathy in action. Presently, this nation could use a huge dose of anti-apathy. Voter turnout numbers for the last several elections are indicative that our society is heavily infested with political apathy.

Less than Good

"If it ain't broke, don't fix it."

Probably everyone has heard this argument: certainly our government has its faults, but it's not *that* bad. Especially compared to other governments around the world. And if things are not *that* bad, why should anyone complain about the status quo?

Indeed, we should all be happy – satisfied with things as they are.

Those of us who are not happy and feel that change and improvement are necessary in our government *do not find fault with our* **system of government***, rather, we find fault with the* **governmental systems***.* What I mean by **governmental systems** are those impractical practices, cumbersome processes and worn out procedures, including much of the misguided methodology which has been not only created but perpetuated over time by career politicians. These entrenched and legislatively protected **governmental systems** give rise to a number of our nation's political embarrassments. How about political credibility? How about believability in the effectiveness of our government? How about the corruption and greed of our elected officials?

These wrongs and/or doubts hinder rather than enhance our democratic form of government and our political system in general.

Card carrying members of the Democratic Party or the Republican Party are pleased with the current state of our government. These people should be pleased. They view those of us who are less than satisfied with present governmental systems with contempt and disbelief. Their systems are working and working well (for them) — why change anything, they ask? They are happy and no wonder!

Change, political or otherwise, is not made by happy, contented people.

Our system of government is excellent - our governmental systems are foul!

Bribery, Corruption and Greed

Our democracy, over time, has become polluted by corruption and greed - in short - bribery. The legislative process and the political systems controlling it have been reduced to mere commodities to be bought by the highest bidder and sold or traded for the greatest price. Were the United States of America just another banana republic, perhaps systematized bribery could be understood as an acceptable practice. However, for the greatest nation on earth, bribery is a pollution within our system of government that is perpetuated by governmental systems. Uninhibited greed by politicians and the major political parties, and their nonchalance about this corruption, is a national disgrace and an international embarrassment. That politics and politicians are equated with crime and corruption by the children of this nation is inexcusable. Elected officials should serve as role models for the future generation. How terrible it is that politicians are for sale.

Political action committees, lobbyists and the corrupt in corporate America, along with all other special interests, are in fact in the business of bribery of public officials. Call it what you will, those spreading around "soft money" are involved in systematized bribery - payoffs of our elected officials. This foul system is perpetuated and protected by allowance. This practice goes on without shame or remorse by those involved. The practice is necessary, they contend, to get things done politically. And really, the wording surrounding the bribery of public officials sounds pretty nice. "Soft money," "lobbying," "political action committee money," "special interest funds" and other terms which sound much less sinister than bribery, corruption and payoffs are all in vogue in an attempt to legitimatize influence peddling. How nice!?!

Really?

To be sure, not all of our politicians are taking bribes. However, were just one crooked politician accepting one bribe, this, (in the opinion of those of us who want this contemptible practice ended) is one bribe too many. Politicians who sell themselves and the interests of those whom they are elected to represent for a price are no better than those practicing "the world's oldest profession." It may even be that the politicians accepting bribes are worse. Prostitutes are only selling their bodies, while politicians taking bribes are selling their souls, their integrity and any semblance of morality. The primary difference, perhaps, between those practicing the world's oldest profession and the politicians who are on the take is that the prostitutes and pimps are at least honest and up front about their means of enrichment.

Decisions made concerning legislation and public law have far too great an effect on the lives of all citizens in a democracy to reduce these decisions to the level of *a commodity* to be *bought and sold at market*. Those who enjoy speaking in this strange language of euphemisms have nice clean-sounding ways to describe the practice. Nevertheless, this bribery, which allegedly helps with the decision making process, is systematized corruption of government.

Systematic bribery must be ended and NOW!

In 2001 a member of the Republican Party (Senator John McCain - R -AZ), in conjunction with a member of the Democratic Party (Senator Russ Feingold - D - WI), made an attempt to put a stop to campaign finance corruption. The bill was passed and went into effect in November of 2002. However, by the time the bill was passed, it had little to do with the original intent of the legislation introduced. In its final form, there were so few teeth left in the bill that it needed dentures. Imagine that! A bill to put a stop to the bribery involved in campaign finance reduced to a shadow of its original intent. Nice try guys!

The final form of the weakened bill that was passed through the legislative process is a perfect example of the pathetic results achieved when working through an entrenched government system — a system that will not be done away with by members of either of the major political parties. Too much is at stake for them. The resulting political favoritism based on political contributions is an injustice to our system of government no matter how it is done or under what euphemistic label it is practiced.

BRIBERY IS BRIBERY! IT HAS NO PLACE IN THE POLITICAL ARENA OR IN OUR DEMOCRATIC SYSTEM OF GOVERNMENT IN THE UNITED STATES OF AMERICA!

Shouldn't putting an end to the practice of bribery fall primarily to the membership of the Democratic Party? After all, are they not the party who purports to represent the poor — those who, since they have no money, can have no voice in government systems that are for sale to the highest bidder? What can the poor use to bid for political favoritism? The champions of the poor – the Democrats – point the accusing finger at the Republicans, blaming them and their rich supporters for the initiation of this awful practice, while contending that they must continue their own corrupt practices just to keep up with their more corrupt Republican rivals. The practice is continued, argue the Democrats, because without their participation only the Republicans' rich constituents would benefit.

If government is only for sale to the rich, and the rich are represented by the Republican Party, doesn't it follow that the best course of action for the Democratic Party would be to initiate legislation which would outlaw this corrupt practice, thereby protecting the interests of those who cannot afford to pay to have their voices heard? Yeah, right!

How many millionaire politicians of either party sincerely care about the well being of the poor? Is it just possible that appearing to champion the cause of the poor is nothing more than an excuse to continue the political gridlock while playing the blame game?

The fact is that the membership of neither of the major political parties is clean on this issue of bribery. Both parties play the blame game and continue the finger pointing and name calling. Nothing changes. The systematized bribery continues.

The primary purpose of bribery in politics is political fund raising to build the war chests for political election or reelection campaigns. Bribery has become the main tool by which to implement and perpetuate the corruption surrounding the governmental system of tenured seniority, which equates to political power and influence.

Tenure

Much of the corruption in our government can be attributed to the system of tenure in office of our elected officials. Members of both parties take bribes to perpetu-ate their seniority in office or this system of tenure. Poli-ticians are happily entrenched in a system that rewards seniority rather than ingenuity, innovation, creativity and vision. Because of the tenure system, politicians know they will be reelected by their constituents, not because of their efforts to do good or make a positive difference for the nation or their districts, but rather, because their constituents can ill afford to forfeit any given politician's position of seniority, and therefore power. Given the tenure system as it now exists, any state or region repre-sented by a newly elected congressman or senator loses the power as well as the prestige and the influence that go hand in hand with systematized seniority or tenure. This system of political seniority has resulted in arrogance on the part of many elected officials, who feel themselves to be above the laws other citizens must abide by. Known crooks and worse are reelected to protect any given elec-torate's congress person's or senator's seniority because, in so doing, the electorate preserves this tenure and the political power derived from this seniority system.

The system of tenured power and the corruption surrounding it must be brought to an end!

Did the Founding Fathers ever envision representation of a populace as a career? Wasn't public service to be viewed as a temporary privilege rather than a lifelong career?

While it might be true that 80- and 90-year-old elected officials with several decades of tenure make for great legend and lore, might it just also be possible that relic legislators with nearly a half century of elected office occupation are not among the most innovative, energetic and creative representatives of the people? In the case of many of these antique legislators, complacency has compromised creativity in legislation. The high comfort levels of tenured office holders, plodding along within time-worn routines and systems, stand in the way of innovation for the public good. Fixed mind sets do not produce vision.

Elected officials should be about affecting positive change for the citizenry through legislation – they should *not* be about legend and lore.

The Inverted Triangle

In a democracy, the flow of power can be viewed as a triangle, with the *power sent upwards* to the elected few at the peak *from the broad citizen base.* Elected representatives are to receive their power from the people. Tenure, with the accompanying arrogance and hypocrisy that results from these secure, protected positions, has inverted the intended power flow. The situation at present is that the power flows downward from the few on top to the many at the base.

This inversion of the flow of power is a perversion of one of the most basic principles of democracy.

Has the power of the citizen base been allowed to diminish by an apathetic, lazy citizenry, as a matter of convenience, lack of initiative, or both?

Probably.

The common attitude seems to be, "Oh well, what can I do about it? I can't change a thing." This certainly becomes a self-fulfilling prophecy when citizens are willing to accept such statements as truth.

Only the concentrated efforts of a third major political party with a new political view, agenda and philosophy can affect any change to an entrenched system of political tenure and the resulting comfort and arrogance of those who perpetuate such a system.

Credibility

Who believes much of what is said by our politicians anymore? **Who?**

Only the very gullible or those who are on the receiving end of a benefits package provided by elected officials (so called entitlement programs) care to listen to politicians anymore.

Few of us who must pay believe politicians anymore.

And speaking of paying . . .

Cumbersome, Complex Tax Laws

Is our system of taxation fair to all of our citizens? Is our taxation policy just confusing enough, because of the complexity of the tax laws, to cause a sense of hopelessness? Could the tax laws possibly be made more complex? If so, who would benefit? Could it be that the volume and intricacy of these tax laws result in a level of frustration which will force anyone other than a CPA to simply give up when trying to make sense of them? Under these conditions then, will public apathy continue to insure that nothing changes in our system of taxation?

Is it possible to change these laws so that average, tax-paying citizens can understand the tax laws and accept the responsibility of paying taxes as part of their citizenship? The present system of taxation and the laws governing taxation need to be reviewed, refined, simplified and cleaned up. Public frustration and apathy continue to be the reason for maintenance of the status quo

Wings

Left wing. Right wing. The Responsible Party is going to have neither a right wing nor a left wing. Unlike the current two major political parties, we will have our feet planted firmly on the ground. We will observe and listen to the circling (they are forced to circle with only one wing or the other) vultures overhead with their single wing flapping nearly as fast as their mouths. We will believe that the political posture of either of the "winged" parties is equally foolish, silly, reckless, irresponsible and by definition - unbalanced.

Our understanding of these single wing growths boils down to the idea that only a right wing or only a left wing are merely strange growths – mutations that form when fed by pervasive and irresponsibly wild demonstrations of passion in the absence of good reasoning and sound practicality.

While it is certainly a virtue to be passionate about political involvement, passion for right wing or left wing politics, along with the resulting corruption presently built into our system, need *not* have *any* role in the decision making surrounding the legislative process.

Instead, sound reasoning, rational, results-driven decision making, coupled with studied analysis of realistic models, all of which emanate from a deep sense of responsibility, need to become the course of action, the new direction to take with regard to the political decision-making process. At present, rationality, results-driven decision making, careful reasoning and analysis *do not* seem to be considered worthwhile criteria for making the legislative decisions which affect the lives of all American citizens.

Presently, the sense of responsibility regarding the legislative decision-making process seems to end with emotionalism and extremism. Additionally, the rhetoric of political campaigns for reelection, and the resulting political contributions which lead directly to the fattened wallets of those accepting the bribes used to perpetuate the system, constitute "responsible government" in the view of far too many of our elected officials.

It has been made clear to me on numerous occasions that the list of great political *moderates* would be a short list indeed. In the past, only those politicians with either a passionate commitment to *radical liberalism* or *radical conservatism* have been the politicians who have gained historical notoriety in this country. Too Bad!

What if, instead of labeling a political position as either radically liberal or radically conservative, either left wing or right wing, we identified a third option – a "let's take a practical look" position – so that we could arrive at a new label, a different terminology for politicians who wish to identify themselves with neither of the warring camps? What if we did away with the label of moderate or centrist which all too often really means lacking the guts to identify with either radical liberals or conservatives? What if we, as citizens, championed those politicians who are passionate about their **sound judgment?** Their **wisdom?** Their refusal to indulge in knee-jerk political reactions? Politicians who are noteworthy because they possess a marvelous sense of **reason?** Who have a great passion for **practicality?** Who are **results oriented** and study proposed legislation in enough depth to view legislative bills not merely as "quick fixes" for short term problems, but rather understand that there just may be other considerations beyond the obvious, present needs for remedy? What if we came to value those passionately committed to their **integrity?** Could or would our nation's voting citizens come to value such an individual or group of individuals? How about making this sort of change so that rather than label a politician who is neither liberal nor conservative as "moderate," could we, instead, label such elected officials as *"reasonable"* or *"responsible"* or *"practical?"*

The time is long past due to put an end to legislative decision making based on passion!

It is true that one cannot be passionately "moderate." My critics have made a proper call in this regard. However, these same critics are tied to the political ideas of the past and have no vision and little if any interest in political change in the future. It is, however, very true that politicians could be quite passionate about being reasonable or responsible or practical or of sound judgment or all of the above. To be politically passionate about these new labels would be worthwhile. We must reject the idea and label of "moderate" if we, as a new political party, wish to have and use labels which will appeal to the voting public.

As an example of the preceding concept, let me offer up the following ongoing and emotionally charged issue: forests land use. On the one hand we have the environmentalist groups who believe that forests should be allowed to grow to maturity and the trees be left to die of old age then to fall over and rot on the forest floor. They believe strictly in pristine forest conditions. In certain areas and in certain forests, this group has a very valid point. However, this thinking does not logically fit with all forest situations. Yet, emotionally charged environmentalists (for political posturing purposes) demand that the pristine forest viewpoint be the only approach to all forests in all situations. Is this reasonable?

On the other hand, loggers and lumber industry groups want to see "clear cutting" practices flourish due primarily to economic factors. They argue (and establish their political position) that due to the competitive nature of the industry and the need to supply the market with abundant and inexpensive building materials, they need to be allowed to use the most inexpensive methods to harvest the forests. Never mind what "clear cutting" does to promote erosion, denude the land, etc., etc. Is this industry posturing reasonable?

The responsible approach to this widely divided issue of the practical use of our nations forests is to incorporate the forestry practice of "select harvesting" wherein forest products are made available to the market while at the same time the forest is not ravaged and the forested area is not laid waste. Neither of the original opposition sides will be totally pleased with this more reasonable and responsible approach to their radically opposed viewpoints, but the general public will be best served which should always be the point in political confrontations. Selective harvesting will certainly increase the costs to consumers of forest based products but this cost will be offset by reduced public expenditures on reforestation and erosion damage repair.

Stalemate

Watching the FOX NEWS program "Hannity & Colmes" is not unlike watching our legislative branch of government in action given the present two party system. Listening to Sean Hannity, a staunch conservative, argue with the ultra liberal Allen Colmes is not at all unlike listening to members of the two parties do battle in the House of Representatives or the Senate. Both usually involve nothing more than a series of excuses, denials, finger pointing, name calling, and blame-game activities, which have resulted in impasse, stalemate and gridlock. Nothing gets accomplished, blame is always placed on the other side of the aisle, responsibilities are denied, and the name calling and labeling continues for reasons noteworthy only to career politicians. At least the "Hannity & Colmes" program is a form of entertainment, whereas government stalemate is a national disgrace. Views on issues are polarized, entrenched, cemented and never, ever changed. Rarely have we ever, either on television or in the halls of government, heard a conservative say to a liberal, or vice-versa, "You know what? I have to go along with you on this one. You are right. You've convinced me. I agree."

Since stalemate pervades the legislative process, perhaps we should just send the membership of the House and the Senate home and let Sean Hannity and Allen Colmes handle issues surrounding political debates. Accomplishments, or lack thereof, would likely be equal to or greater than what goes on in the legislative process at present. Impasse would continue, decisions (if any), or indecision (certainly), would take less time with only two people arguing. Just think of the cost savings to us all.

Another View

The Responsible Party will serve as the gathering place for those who appreciate a common sense approach to politics and government. The general membership and party

members elected to office will take the reasonable, responsible, practical approach to issues – the logical, realistic,
results-oriented approach so rare in present day politics.
Emotion and passion will not be involved in the decision-
making process. As such, there will be times when a more
liberal view will make the most sense, and other times when
the more conservative position will be the one of choice for
Responsible Party members - **but radical conservatism or liberalism - never!**

A built-in problem concerning the "moderate" political stance (to use the presently accepted terminology)
is that this centrist position requires, even mandates,
that there continue to be ultra liberals as well as ultra
conservatives to allow Responsible Party elected officials to maintain our non-passion-driven position, at
least initially. While Responsible Party members would
do battle with either side of the aisle or both, the presence of both major parties is necessary to our very
existence. Perhaps preservation of the right wing and
the left wing is not so bad after all. While the major

parties continue flapping their single wings and mouths, The Responsible Party will maintain a firmly grounded position and make the sensible, logical, results-oriented decisions that can and will do the greatest good for the greatest number of American citizens.

III. Another Party?

The Constitution of the United States of America states that there shall be **three** separate branches of government for the expressed purpose of a creating a balance of power. Is it not reasonable, therefore, that this same **three-way**, balance-of-power concept should be made available to the citizens regarding their choice of affiliation with political parties and their philosophies? Three major operational political parties would insure that a true balance of power existed in the legislative process.

What possible good could come of organizing another political party? After all, at present, there are some 50 political parties already registered, in existence and operating in the United States of America today.

Why one more?

Name a U. S. senator or congressman that does not belong to either the Democratic Party or the Republican Party. There may be one independent, but only one.

Name a U. S. President that does not belong to either the Republican Party or the Democratic Party. You need to go way back in our nation's history to a time before the Republican Party was formed, when there was a Whig Party. Millard Fillmore was the last Whig to hold the office of the presidency. George Washington was of no party. Other than Washington, Fillmore, and a few other Whigs, all of the other presidents of this nation have been members of either the Democratic or the Republican Party.

Other than the Republican Party and the Democratic Party, no existing party is making any sort of difference politically for American citizens. While others do exist, they accomplish nothing other than producing a voice of dissent. Given the numbers of popular votes for all of these third parties combined, those voices of dissent are barely heard.

Therefore, organize a new party. Start with a clean, fresh approach.

Wouldn't it be possible to simply make changes within the existing structure, or focus or mission of any one of the existing non-major parties already in operation? This is a fair question.

Have you ever taken even a peripheral view of the platforms of any of the existing non-Democratic or non-Republican parties presently found on local, state and national ballots? There are radical socialists, radical environmentalists, radical gun control people, radical agriculture advocates, radical labor, radical this and radical that - but certainly radical all. There are neo-Nazis, communists, pro-life, pro-abortion, even pro-pot parties for your choosing. You may choose to become a member of either a radical left wing or a radical right wing party but not of a party advocating nothing more radical than a common sense approach. Choices abound for those who are not content with the politics of either of the two major parties. It would seem that there is something for everyone, from those who seek a legalized high to those who feel armed insurrection is the only way to make change within our democracy. Certainly, all of these parties have their limited followings. However, not one of these parties is affecting any real change for the betterment of our nation's government or our political system. Not one of these third parties represents the interests of those who feel that the common sense political position is the one that makes the most sense for the most citizens.

A clean, fresh start for a clean, fresh, new political party seems to be the only logical answer to making positive change a reality in our nation. This new third party will not be a radical splinter group advocating a new social order. Rather, its focus will be to seek to remedy the foulness entrenched in our governmental systems. The effort of the party will be directed towards ending the corrupt systems inherent in the present two-party format, which are and will remain out of control without a new challenge to their perpetuation. The new party's elected members will seek to end the political impasse. Party leadership will strive for **a new political direction, innovation**, and **real world results** *rather than just more political rhetoric.*

Face the facts. The leaders as well as the membership of the two major political parties are very happy with the status quo. Why would they change current governmental systems when things are going just the way they would have it? What's to clean up? What is wrong with 80- to 90-year-olds making public policy and growing old while in office? What do you mean by talking of bribery? What is wrong with getting a little help from paid political operatives when legislative decisions need to be made? Everything is just fine!

Corrupt systems must be ended permanently and promptly. Corrupt individuals must be held account-able. Morality, ethics and basic human decency within government must be restored.

Just as a baker gets rid of the product that has been on the shelf for too long, and the produce manager throws out the less-than-fresh fruit and vegetables, we too should rid ourselves of those who have wasted the opportunity to improve the lives of those they serve. Stale bakery should not occupy the same shelf as the fresh. Rotting produce spoils the fresh placed next to it. Likewise, how can stale or rotten policy makers possibly make these United States a better place for its citizenry? It is a good thing that we can't smell the foulness of rotting or stale politics made possible by a system of tenured political office. But smell or no smell, we can certainly **see** the effects of spoiled politicians.

Will the membership of either the Republican or the Democratic Parties seek to put an end to the system of tenured office? **NEVER! IT WON'T HAPPEN!** Why should they? Both parties are perfectly happy to perpetuate a system that promotes ineffective political leadership and results in political stalemate, gridlock and impasse.

But what if elected candidates knew they had a limited time in which to make a positive difference for their constituents? What if it were a fact that at the end of a given time frame these politicians knew they would step down? Stagnation would be unthinkable. Real effort would need to be put forth by politicians to make as much of a positive difference as possible within the constraints of the time allowed them. Perhaps even their first priority, after being sworn into office, would be to make positive change rather than concentrating on raising funds for their reelection campaign. Wouldn't that be an idea? Under the present tenure system, it seems fund raising is priority one. Under the present tenure system, public service is not viewed as a job to be done, but rather as a career for life if enough funds can be raised.

Only the founding of a new major political party with a fresh start and fresh ideas can affect change. Those who have lost their ethics in the maze of tenured politics will never put an end to the entrenched, corrupted systems they have created and protected and with which they are so shamelessly comfortable.

If term limits were in effect, those individuals determined to continue with a political career after their term in any given elected office is finished could seek office with either a move up, or a move down in the political hierarchy. **But certainly, they would be forced to move on and move out!**

Another Party?

If the President of the United States of America can only serve for a limited time, why should all elected officials not be subject to the same type of rule?

IV. Looking Back

Looking back on the activities of third parties during the 20th century makes an interesting study. Only once did just less than 1 in 3 voters vote for the third party candidate. Once, just less than 1 in 5 voted for the third party candidate. Twice, right around 1 in 8 voted for the third party candidate. Never, other than those four times out of the 25 national elections held during the 20th century, did third party voting make even the slightest difference. But why?

A brief review of history shows us that during the early years of the 20th century, political unrest, due primarily to agricultural price declines, gave rise to third party voting. The 1912 election, when Theodore Roosevelt ran on the Progressive Party (Bull Moose) ticket, was nothing more than a personal vendetta waged by Roosevelt against President William Howard Taft. Even though he was Roosevelt's handpicked successor, Taft did not carry out the programs Roosevelt wanted, so Roosevelt attacked his one- time friend with a vengeful third party run for the presidency. Roosevelt's third party run resulted in the election of Woodrow Wilson. The 1912 election results for Roosevelt hold the record for the greatest percentage of popular votes ever cast for a third party candidate — an amazing 27.39%.

The second best showing after Roosevelt belongs to H. Ross Perot in his 1992 presidential run. Perot captured just over 19% of the popular vote. Perot called his party the Reform Party. But unfortunately, Perot *was* the party, and after he no longer was involved with it, the Reform Party, like most 20th century third parties, simply faded away.

Third place belongs to Robert La Follette and his Progressive Party run for the presidency in the election of 1924. La Follette captured 16.56% of the popular vote.

Fourth place belongs to George Wallace and his American Independent Party in his 1968 bid for the presidency. Unbelievably, the segregationist Wallace received 13.53% of the popular vote.

Other than John Anderson, an independent, who took 6.61 % of the popular vote in the 1980 election, all other attempts by third parties for national office have resulted in, at best, around 3% or less of the popular vote.

All of these third party attempts have involved a run for the presidency of the United States, with little if any sustained effort expended on runs at House or Senate seats, let alone state and local runs.

There remains one interesting political phenomenon concerning third party voting and candidates for office during the 20th century. Minnesota actually elected independent Reform Party candidate Jesse Ventura as governor in 1998.

Governor Ventura, while an interesting political anomaly, is indicative of what can and will happen to all elected third party candidates without the support of other members of the legislature who share their political philosophy. Without the critical support of other party members in the legislature, third party candidates elected to leadership positions are doomed to ineffectiveness from the start of their terms in office. As in the case of Governor Ventura, a few pieces of legislation brought forth by the elected leader are passed initially, during the honeymoon period. But after a few initial legislative successes, members of both major political parties did everything in their power to make certain that Governor Ventura was constantly reminded that he was not a member in good standing of either of their parties. Though a non-Republican, non-Democrat may well have great ideas and good intentions, as did Governor Ventura, and may, as a matter of fact, have been elected by popular vote, without the support of fellow party members in the legislative branch, any third party political leader will be rendered completely ineffective by both Democrats and Republicans who control the legislative branch of government.

Ventura's election campaign was fun to observe. He offered up some interesting ideas concerning taxation as well as other novel ideas for his legislative agenda. At the candidates' debate forum, Jesse Ventura basically sat there listening to his political rivals pound on one another. He said very little. Both of the candidates he faced had their own problems, and Ventura really didn't need to say much. He shrewdly let the two major party candidates kill each other off. One of those major players had all of the charm, personality, and charisma of a brick, while the other had some political baggage (he switched parties for a run at the governor's office) that left the voters doubting him. Ventura's basic appeal to the voters was this: "Look, if you don't want either of these babbling idiots to head up your state government, I'll do it."

Ventura's strategy worked.

After his election, Governor Ventura was allowed by the legislature to restructure Minnesota's motor vehicle license plate fee schedule and establish a mass transit system called the Light Rail Transit System. This mass transit system had been talked about for years but never acted upon in the legislature. Both Republicans and Democrats feared this mass transit system just might become a political pariah; therefore, not one member of either of the major parties had the guts to initiate or back the legislation to make the system happen. Once Governor Ventura of the Reform Party demonstrated the guts, drive, vision and courage to initiate the legislation to make the Light Rail Transit System a reality, members of both major parties backed the legislation, hoping its passage would kill Governor Ventura politically. But the Republican Party and their Democratic Party co-conspirators got it wrong.

It turns out that the Light Rail Transit System is a tremendous success story in the Minneapolis and St. Paul metropolitan area of Minnesota. As a matter of fact, this mass transit system is such a success story that many of the suburban metro area communities want to be linked into the system. Nothing would have come of this marvelous mass transit system success story had it not been for Governor Ventura's leadership. The Twin Cities' Light Rail Transit System stands as this nation's lone tribute to a third party politician with the courage, vision and integrity to make a positive difference for the populace he was elected to serve.

After the passage of the Twin Cities mass transit development program legislation, even with appeals to the populace who elected him, Governor Ventura was unable to affect further change. Democrats and

Republicans joined forces to place roadblocks in the path of any further legislative initiatives by the governor. Legislative innovation and creativity that might have taken place under the governor's leadership were thwarted by members of both the major parties in the state legislature for fear that other of the governor's ideas might have merit as well, which would leave major party candidates vulnerable in the next election. Here, then, is a rare situation in which members of both of the major political parties joined forces to work together for the sole purpose of rendering a real leader powerless. Their combined purpose was to eliminate any further legislative vision, initiative and creativity on the part of the elected third party official. After all, the problem for the major parties was that even though they did not know at the time how successful any of the governor's other ideas might or might not be, they couldn't take the risk that his ideas might have merit, or worse yet, make a positive difference in the lives of the citizens of Minnesota. Fear in both of the major party circles allowed for no further successful legislation. Could the members of both major political parties perhaps have been afraid that another legislative success by the governor would have caused voting citizens to take another look at the viability of third party candidates?

Governor Ventura became the target of a media feeding frenzy when he started to referee wrestling matches and became a commentator for football games after being cut out of the political process by the Republicans and Democrats in the Minnesota state legislature. After being made to look like a buffoon by critics in both major parties, and then by the media besides, why would he not choose to do something else, since his power to affect change for the state had been thwarted by those who were seeking to preserve the status quo?

Governor Ventura's legacy will not go away. He stands alone as the one bright shining star that broke into the system. For those of us who hold that a new direction and a new third party need to become a reality, Minnesota's Governor Jesse Ventura is a true hero.

Of all the 20th century's third party candidates, only one could have pushed through any of his programs and legislative initiatives — Theodore Roosevelt. At the time he ran as a third party candidate, he was well known to both the general population of the country as well as many of the legislators serving in the Senate and the House. Through the force of his will, his dynamic personality and his immense popularity, the 26th president could have affected positive change through popular appeal. Theodore Roosevelt alone might have been successful, had he become the first ever third party candidate elected to the presidency. (Had T. R. not declared that he would not seek reelection after his elected term was completed, he would have more likely than not been reelected as a Republican.)

To summarize, the justification for formation of a new third party is that the full weight of a party organization is needed to back any elected leader. Elected leaders need the company of other members of their party who share the same philosophy and vision of the future. Legislative change cannot be made to happen by a single individual without the support and backing of like-minded party members on the floor of the legislature.

No elected official should need to suffer through a term of office without being able to affect at least some change. Governor Ventura's record of legislative stalemate for most of his term in office serves as the only example we can call on to demonstrate what happens to non-Republican or non-Democratic Party members elected as leaders but without support in the legislature. Governor Ventura had noble intentions and some very innovative and creative ideas. But in the end, one individual without political party backing in the legislature can do little to affect much-needed change.

Can you imagine how effective four years of the leadership of President H. Ross Perot might have been, given that there would have been 535 major party members in the legislature devoting all their time and energy to making sure that President Perot was "hog tied" during his term in office?

V. Looking Ahead

In the absence of a major third party, political gridlock and stalemate can and will continue. There are those citizens who are delighted by the prospect of just such a scenario — they are card-carrying members of either the Republican or Democratic Parties.

Then there are those of us who are not happy with political impasse. We want to see change. We want to see changing faces representing us. We want to see an end to the system of tenured office. We want an end to the rampant bribery and corruption. We want simplified tax laws. We want stand-alone legislation so that we can, once and for all, know what our representatives are voting for or against on our behalf.

Actions taken by a third major party will end stalemate and force political movement. Political coalitions will need to be formed once there are three parties, not two, representing the electorate on the floor of the House and Senate. The political wrangling of three parties will take the place of bribery and payoffs. Two against one legislative coalitions will be formed to enact any and all legislation. True political posturing and real negotiation (not bribery and payoffs) can and will be the result of the demise of the "good old boys club" which is enabled by the tenure system.

It will be impossible for members of the existing major parties to simply dismiss members of a third major party. Rather than being ignored or brushed aside, elected third party members will need to be, must be by necessity, "courted" in all of the decision making processes by members of both of the existing major political parties.

When there is a third major political party with elected officials at all levels of government, the members of that third party should and will caucus before every legislative vote. The third party will agree on its position as a party on any given issue. At that point, taking a responsible position on an issue based on results-oriented, fact-driven, rational choices, the position of the third party caucus will side with either the liberals or the conservatives to force the issue. Better yet will be the time when legislation introduced by The Responsible Party takes the solidly founded, reasonable, responsible, middle-of-the-road, common sense position. The Responsible Party's position can then attract the support of members of the two major political parties. Leaving aside the radical extreme members of the two major political parties, it will be both interesting and fun to watch members of either major party be forced to admit that moderation and sound judgment can actually make the best possible positive difference in the lives of the citizens of our nation.

Real political action made necessary by political co-alitions will cause change. Only a third major political party can affect this much-needed change, which will spell the demise of the existing political stalemate and impasse.

We will have our own party, our own candidates, our own platform and our own political agenda. We will be a political force to be dealt with!

VI. Formation and Organization of the Responsible Party

It will be much easier to form a new major political party in the early part of the 21st century than it was in the late 19th or early 20th centuries. Ease of communications alone will make it far simpler to get a new party up and running. Much of the organizational work can be accomplished by FAX or telephone, and the internet will make our job even easier. Founders of previously organized third parties could only dream of the speed and efficiency we will bring to creation of the Responsible Party.

The Responsible Party will set up an office and create a Web site to facilitate membership application. This general office will be the national clearing house and serve as coordinator for all party activities on national, state and local levels. We will staff our office with professional individuals so that organizational meetings and other pertinent party meetings and events can be effectively scheduled and monitored. The Responsible Party will issue membership cards and party pins to paying members, and a monthly newsletter will keep our membership informed of party activities, actions and results.

The Responsible Party membership will understand that we will need political operatives on the national, state, county and local levels. Without this multi-layered activity on the part of the Responsible Party, we know that we can have no long-term effect on the American political process. Without these various tiers of political involvement, we understand that we too will end up on the list of those parties who were here today, gone tomorrow.

Our vision, our goal, is to become a long-term, major presence on the American political landscape. Ours will not be a party of one formed for a one-time run at the presidency.

Each state (and each county or metropolitan area in densely populated areas) will form a local party organization. Local leadership will be elected on each level. National and state meetings will be held once a year (more often if necessary), with delegates attending from each of the various local party organizations.

The Responsible Party will establish a party platform consisting initially of four or five planks — no more. As a party, at national meetings, we will establish a responsible position with regard to pressing issues of the day — those issues not specifically addressed in our party platform. We will, however, never lose site of the main focus points contained within our platform planks. By keeping our party platform position simple, we will *not* follow the example of the existing two major parties. The Responsible Party will *not* attempt to be "all things to all people." By so doing, The Responsible Party will take a solid political stand, while the two major parties, because of the complexity of their platforms, really stand for nothing at all and represent nobody serious about real issues.

Over time, as our platform agenda issues are resolved in our favor, we will establish new platform planks that our membership feels are in the best interest of the nation, states, counties and the party. But always, we will keep our party platform clean and simple. Our platform will have solid but few planks. This nation's citizens, Responsible Party members or not, will always be able to understand the political planks, platform, positions and agenda of the Responsible Party.

We need to get our organizational meetings under way — either face to face or over the internet — in order to make the Responsible Party a reality.

VII. Membership Criteria

Many of the signers of the Declaration of Independence went on to become the warriors who made possible the founding of this great nation. Those who fought to bring about this "great political experiment" had had enough of armed conflict. When it came time to write the Constitution of the United States of America, many of these same great leaders made provision for change in the government, all within the limits of the constitution and **without resorting to armed conflict.**

There are those in our nation today who advocate government change by armed insurrection. A number of these splinter groups — survivalists and other crackpots — operate throughout these United States. These individuals must be illiterate, for were they able to read and understand the history of this nation and our constitution, they would soon come to realize that provision has been made for nonviolent change within our government. The real battleground for political change in the United States of America lies not in the streets but in the hearts and minds of a politically motivated populace.

The Responsible Party does not seek as members those of the "lunatic fringe."

Even the great visionaries of the past, our founding fathers, advocated change now and then as the need arose. Thomas Jefferson said, "A little rebellion now and then is a good thing, and as necessary in the political world as storms in the physical." George Washington said in this regard, "The happiness of nations can be accomplished by pacific revolutions in their political systems without the destructive intervention of the sword." Change can be accomplished in this nation **without armed conflict,** if we are smart enough to read and heed what the Founding Fathers wrote. The Responsible Party does *not* want members who believe that violence is the only way to bring about political change. We recognize that our fight is a war against apathy and our battle plan is to bring political indifference to an end.

Both of the existing major parties seem to have the answers for many members of our society. So many citizens seem satisfied to adopt, without question, the political position of the major parties. Life is simple. The party says (whatever), so that is my position. I don't have to think; I don't even need to look at the issues — the party has it all figured out for me. I'm a Democrat or I'm a Republican and that's all I need to know. Perhaps non-thinkers make the most ideal party members. If so, The Responsible Party will want no ideal members.

THE RESPONSIBLE PARTY

The Responsible Party will be of no use to people who are incapable of thinking. The Responsible Party is not looking for robots to fill our membership rolls.

The Responsible Party membership will be made up of those who are not satisfied with the political positions of either of the existing major political parties. Responsible Party members will be thinkers and visionaries who want to right the wrongs of our governmental systems.

Party members will be those who have the courage not only to speak up, but to stand up for what they believe they can change for the better. Party members will be activists for change. Responsible Party members will not be satisfied to wink at continued governmental corruption.

The Responsible Party will seek to enlist members who believe in a high standard of morality and ethics. Party candidates of lesser moral fiber would likely fall into the same political abyss of corruption into which those presently representing the existing major parties have fallen.

The Responsible Party is not an organization intent on perpetuating systematized governmental corruption. We intend to end it.

The Responsible Party will view lack of political experience as a positive trait for those members who seek elected office. Those who don't know the system are more likely to cause change than those who are comfortable within the system.

The avoidance of political entrapment by special interest groups and purveyors of soft money will be as difficult an assignment as could be asked of any mortal. Yet, there are those in our society (and necessarily within the membership of the Responsible Party) who are equal to the task. We need party members whose morals are above reproach to seek elected office if we are to positively end, once and for all, the systematized corruption presently found in government systems. Only those of the highest moral character and virtue can possibly affect positive change within our government system.

Elected Responsible Party members who are caught accepting bribes, payoffs or other forms of graft and corruption will be immediately expelled from the party. They will then be free to join either of the major parties or form a new party of their own (suggested titles: "Bribery is Us" or "Favors for Sale" or "Graft is Good Government").

Let the crooks, cheats and liars join the existing major parties. They will be made to feel right at home with either their right or left winged friends. After all, "birds of a feather …"

As members of the Responsible Party, we need to set an example for the generations to come to follow. We need to raise the standards of political office holders by eliminating the corruption that our nation's children presently equate with politicians in general. Responsible Party members, acting in a responsible manner, will understand that public figures live in glass houses. We can affect positive change by carefully considering how our speech and actions will be perceived by the general public, thus setting a proper example. Responsible Party members will police their fellow party members with regard to proper behavior. This self regulation will result in a positive public image regarding the present and future direction of our party, thus ensuring a steady increase in membership.

We need only be guided by one very simple question with regard to our words and our deeds, and that is: **What sort of example am I setting for children?**

Think of how different our political and governmental systems might be had elected members of the Republican and Democratic Parties asked themselves this one simple question!

Thinkers and visionaries — those of high moral character and those capable of the sound reasoning necessary to formulate realistic solutions to our presently fouled governmental systems — need to apply for membership in The Responsible Party. Our members will know that positive change can be affected only by vigorous political activity. Results-oriented political positions will spur the general population to political action. And it is action not apathy that is needed to bring about change. A politically motivated population will at last be interested enough in the workings of government to do all that is needed to affect change in our government.

If our message, our vision and our actions are inspired, political apathy will be ended. Our battle will be won not with weapons, but with a vision for the future that will put an end to the major foes of democracy — political corruption and voter apathy! An end to political corruption will cause citizens who hear our message to vote! Our message needs to be visionary enough to excite and inspire the previously apathetic, irresponsible, non-voting citizen. Voting is, after all, the act of responsible citizens. Voting is a nonviolent act, and yet it wields the power to affect change. Our new political party, with a new direction and a new focus, coupled with a membership comprised of those who seek an end to political corruption and stalemate, is how the Responsible Party will, once and for all, get out the vote.

At long last, the Responsible Party will give the citizens of this nation something and someone *to vote FOR*. Instead of a limited number of voters going to the poles to "pick the lesser of two evils" or to "oust the incumbent" (either individual or party), we will offer an invigorated electorate something *to vote FOR* — a solid program with solid and attainable goals, all for the betterment of all the citizens of this great nation.

VIII. The Political Platform of the Responsible Party

Term Limits

It will be the position of the Responsible Party that all elected government officials will be bound by term limits. Senators (those serving in either state or federal government positions) may serve no more than two six-year terms in office. Representatives (those serving in either state or federal government positions) may serve no more than six two-year terms in office. Presidents, vice presidents, governors and lieutenant governors may serve no more than two four-year terms in office. Judges' time on the bench will be limited as well.

The system of tenured office must be brought to an end. Stagnation, stalemate and general government inaction are the result of the continuation of the system of tenured office. Regularly elected and, therefore, politically motivated, inspired government officials with a limited time to serve in their elected political positions will be, by necessity, a moving force for positive, progressive legislative and legal change.

End Systematized Bribery and Corruption of Public Officials!

Elected government officials accepting bribes along with those offering bribes will be subject to life imprisonment without parole, or some other form of punishment as yet to be determined. There will be no exceptions. No matter the guise under which the bribe is made and no matter the term applied to the bribery scheme, bribery of public officials will be cause for the prosecution of those involved.

Lobbyists will be outlawed because lobbyists are in the business of bribery. There will be no further need of their services and the corruption that they perpetuate through degrading payoffs that reward the less than ethical. Monetary influence peddling is finished.

Legislators must come to understand that if they have no opinion with regard to any given piece of legislation, or if they are not convinced of the validity of an issue, or if they have not been politically sold on a legislative bill, there is an abstain button available for their use when voting. Being politically motivated to vote an issue is called politics. Being paid to vote an issue is bribery. All bribery of public officials will be ended!

<u>Equal (=) Taxation</u>

All will pay their share of taxes based upon an equal percentage of their income. (Read <u>"Flat Tax Revolution: Using a Postcard to Abolish the IRS"</u> by Steve Forbes). The percentage may vary and will be determined by the legislature. Therefore, those who earn more, pay more. However, all will pay an equal percentage of their income.

Business (including all foreign corporations and other foreign business entities) will pay taxes to this government based upon net income which is generated by their operations in the United States of America. There will be no exceptions. There will be no excuses.

All residents, citizens or otherwise, will pay their share. Street people will pay their percentage as will corporate executives. All will pay their share according to their ability to earn.

There will be a national sales tax. (Read "Fair Tax" by Neil Boortz)

Both the "Flat Tax" and "The Fair Tax" have great merit. Both simplify or possibly even eliminate the taxation mess which is, at best, out of control. Both plans deserve study, discussion and perhaps, an amalgamation to create some new form of revenue collection which will be easily understood by all and, therefore, more effective and better accepted by those who must pay. "All are created equal," therefore, all shall be equally taxed (by percentage).

Any business, foreign or domestic, along with their respective executives, claiming to operate for more than three years at a loss (thereby avoiding payment of taxes) will be thoroughly investigated by the Internal Revenue Service.

Stand Alone Legislation and Sunset Laws

Legislative bills will be sent to the floor for ratification or discard based on the content of the legislation. There will be no riders, sub-clauses or amendments, friendly or otherwise. All legislation will stand alone on its own merits.

All legislation will be in effect for a limited time. Legislation will be subject to periodic review. If a given law is found to be of little positive effect, it will die a natural death if not reenacted by majority vote in the legislature.

Sunset laws will result in a continual review and refinement of government law, policy and practice. Review and study of our laws will end stagnation and ineffectiveness in the legislative process.

Direct Election of Candidates

Given the levels of technology today, the antiquated election practices of the past must be put aside in favor of more streamlined methods for electing candidates. Present procedures may or may not elect the candidate who is the choice of the people. Let the people decide and then let the nation abide by that choice.

The reason for the formation of The Responsible Party is to seek an end to the pervasive, systematized corruption presently found in all levels of government! To accomplish this goal, The Responsible Party's platform will contain only five planks that we feel are solutions to the root cause of the corruption we want ended. They are as follows:

1.) Term Limits

2.) End Bribery and Corruption

3.) "=" (Equal) Taxation

4.) Stand Alone Legislation and Sunset Laws

5.) Direct Elections

We will keep our platform simple, basic and free of clutter!

Other issues facing us in the political arena will be dealt with based on establishing a party position rather than political platform planks. We will establish these party positions based on careful thought and the consensus of the various individual local, county and state party organizations, arriving at national party positions to present to the voting public on issues we do not wish to incorporate into our political platform. All Responsible Party Representatives on all levels will follow the identical party line with regard to party policy and positions, regardless of personal opinion or personal agenda, or face expulsion from the party. The solidarity of our positions will result in a party unified by common goals and ideals. We will present to the public a party that knows where it is headed, knows what it wants to accomplish, and knows how to get there.

The Responsible Party will seek positive change while understanding that our priority must remain to free our government of corruption. Government systems which pollute the legislative process must be ended for good. Only then can a true democratic government function as intended by those whose vision made our form of government the envy of every freedom-loving individual in the world.

IX. Early Objectives, Operations and Policies

Initial Phase

First of all, we must begin by attracting like-minded citizens to membership in our newly formed party. These members must, in turn, spread the word regarding our new party — must let others know of our goals and objectives, our vision for the future, and the means and methods by which we plan to meet our goals.

The Responsible Party will have several factors in its favor with regard to creating interest in the movement and recruitment of new members. They are as follows:

1.) Since we are a new party and since we are rejecting the many systematized party practices of the existing parties, our newness, fresh ideas and novel approach to old, tired, bad habits will create excitement in the voting public.

2.) Our members and our office seekers will be energetic proponents of our revisionist version of how government can and should work for the best interests of the most citizens.

3.) Responsible Party members will *seek results rather than expenditure reports* concerning funding of various government sponsored programs. We will accept that spending money is nothing more than a diversionary tactic and an excuse if we have no definitive results to analyze and discuss.

4.) Because the major parties seem satisfied to justify their government-funded programs based on excuses about how much money was spent on other programs, it should be no problem for Responsible Party Candidates to confront major party candidates during elections and ask them to explain what (if anything) was accomplished rather than how much funding has been wasted (certainly).

5.) The Responsible Party will offer a gathering place for those who presently feel they have no representation, no voice in government. The party will be the home base for citizens with a moderate, common sense approach to government rather than the radical approach to politics which we despise.

6.) American citizens will respond favorably to our campaign practices (to be explained under "policies").

7.) Voters, used to seeing candidates on the ballot designated as "Democrat," "Republican," "Libertarian," "Communist," or otherwise, will now be offered a new choice — a candidate designated as "Responsible." This just might encourage some thinking on the part of the voting public.

The internet will probably be our primary tool for promoting awareness of our existence and understanding of the vision and the direction of our party.

Early Operations

Once membership numbers begin to increase, local, county and state party chapters will need to be organized. Party officials at each level will need to be elected.

Local and regional offices as well as a national office will need to be established. The national office should be located in a geographically central area of the country and away from our national capital. While it is true that there will need to be an office in Washington, D. C., this office should never become party headquarters. Establishing the National Headquarters of the Responsible Party away from the national capital will keep party operations cleaner and less apt to be influenced by money and greed. The same holds true for state headquarters — they should never be in the state capitals. Being removed from the polluted, contaminated environment we wish to change will afford the party and its leadership a clearer, cleaner vision for accomplishing our goals.

Every state and local party chapter will need to go through the steps necessary to register the party as a legal political entity so that the Responsible Party can place candidates' names on the election ballot. This will be the first order of business after party chapters are organized and local leadership is elected.

A national meeting of the general membership will need to be held to discuss and then draft the bylaws and operational procedures of the party. Legal counsel will be required to insure the legality of our proceedings.

When we try to become a registered political party, members and especially party leadership will need to understand that we will be stonewalled at every turn by elections officials who are very satisfied with the status quo.

We will not be welcome. However, our persever-ance will win out over those who would prefer that we not exist.

Once on the ballot, we will need to run candidates for office — but not top leadership positions — as soon as possible. We cannot seek top leadership positions until we have established our party members in city councils, county boards, and state and national legisla-tures. We will seek political leadership positions only after we have established some friendly faces in the legislative arena. Without party members in the legislative branch of our government, we can expect nothing but failure for our party members elected to positions of leadership. We will not subject our party members to the humiliation of an unsupported leadership position until and unless we are assured that we have the momentum necessary to elect party members to the floor of the legislature

Party Policies - The High Road

Every party member elected to office will be subjected to all of the bribery and corruption we as a party hope to end. Elected party members will need to document all bribery attempts so that the purveyors of these corrupt practices can be exposed to the public. Although it will be a difficult task to resist the temptation to accept bribes, Responsible Party members elected to office will need to dedicate themselves to the party position of integrity, honesty and decency. The slightest failure to maintain high standards of behavior will bring embarrassment and humiliation on the party and its membership. Rejection of bribery and influence peddling, accepted as common practice today, will take super human effort. Elected Responsible Party members must raise the standards of acceptable moral and ethical behavior for all politicians.

Unfortunately, elected party members will need "to play the game" and go along with many of the legislative processes and systems we wish to end until our elected officeholder numbers increase. Unless they play the game, elected party officials will not be able to effectively serve their constituents. So initially, despite despising the system we wish to eliminate, elected party officials will need to "play ball" with those who perpetuate that system. While this will require tremendous personal discipline on the part of those Responsible Party members elected to office, it will be mandatory for the long term best interests of the party and its constituents.

The campaign tactics of The Responsible Party will "raise the bar" regarding the political campaign practices of the two major political parties. We will not lower ourselves to the level of smear tactics, dirt digging, mudslinging and negativism that is so prevalent in the current political campaign arena.

Responsible Party Candidates will propose a political agenda for the voters' acceptance or rejection based solely on its merits. If these objectives make sense and have validity, voters will choose to vote for The Responsible Party candidates. If the objectives make no sense and lack validity, voters will choose others to represent them. Our candidates will not comment on any other candidate's political position or objectives, other than to say, "I will speak about my program — they will speak about theirs. You decide what makes the most sense to you and vote accordingly."

If our candidates' messages are strong enough, if our ideas and principles are clear enough, if our enthusiasm is contagious enough, if our objectives are worthwhile enough, we will not want or need to resort to negativism in our campaigning.

The Responsible Party will rise above the cesspool of today's major party political campaign practices. We will take the "high road," and Americans want the high road. They are sick of the foulness present in today's major political party campaigns. Instead of trying to distract the voters by criticizing the opposition, our candidates will dwell on the positives of our platform. In so doing, The Responsible Party will set a new standard for conducting political campaigns in The United States of America.

Funding

If it is indeed worthwhile to be a member of The Responsible Party, membership will be worth paying for. Our membership dues may need to be higher than the dues of the other major parties. Following are some justifications for higher membership dues:

1.) Dues will need to fund most party operations.

2.) We will not and cannot allow our party and its principles to be for sale! Lest we fall into the same trap the two major parties find themselves in — bound by all manner of political favors owed to heavy contributors — The Responsible Party *can accept no contributions* from special interest groups or individuals with agendas they wish to promote through influence peddling and bribery. Any contributions to the party will need to be made anonymously. There can be no strings attached to any contributions made to The Responsible Party.

3.) In order for The Responsible Party to promote and maintain the high road with regard to ethics, morals, general integrity and common decency, we are duty bound to fund our operations strictly through membership dues and anonymous donations.

Political Campaign Practices

H. Ross Perot set the example we will follow. He showed how to run a frugal campaign during his 1992 run for the presidency. He didn't have the big bus or the airliner adorned with his name or logo. He wasn't surrounded by an entourage. Perot was not above driving a rented sedan or his own car or flying on commercial flights, and he had no more than three or four people accompany him. Mr. Perot was **the** frugal campaigner. Practical citizens will appreciate a frugal, low budget campaign.

As Responsible Party Members, we must ask ourselves if all is well with America when nearly a billion and a half dollars are spent nationwide on political campaigns during mid-term elections. And to what end? Could those same billions of dollars be put to better use if spent on education, health care, food and shelter for those in need, public works refurbishment, or a whole host of other worthwhile endeavors?

Would it be fair to ask who, if anyone, changes his or her political views based on the hopelessly boring and repetitious political campaign advertisements we are subjected to on television and radio? Are there any American citizens foolish enough to be swayed in their convictions by a recorded political phone message? Is it possible that the message, vision and credibility of a candidate could be more important than the endless repetition of media promotions? Or is it true that the simple repetition of a media blitz is sufficient to overcome lack of credibility for a less-than-forthright candidate?

With regard to political campaign practices, The Responsible Party will stay out of the mud and take the high road. We will conduct our campaigns on a low budget basis — a decision that will be respected by citizens who find the lavish spending of the major party candidates wasteful, extravagant and unjustifiable.

X. Other Considerations

Political Parties should have a mascot or symbol. The Responsible Party is no exception. The Democrats have their jackass, the Republicans their elephant.

The Responsible Party will have as its mascot the Australian Cattle Dog, often referred to as the Australian Blue Heeler. Why choose the Australian Cattle Dog?

Within the chronology of dog breed development, the Australian Cattle Dog is a relatively new breed. With a bluish tint to its coat, this dog works primarily on cattle ranches, where it herds cattle by nipping at their heels.

THE RESPONSIBLE PARTY

The Responsible Party is a new breed of political party, and the Blue Heeler has many of the characteristics that we would like voters to associate with The Responsible Party. For instance, the Heeler is known for its tireless work ethic and its intelligence, resilience, loyalty, toughness and seriousness.

Like our mascot, The Responsible Party will herd the jackasses and elephants, even though they are much larger animals, by nipping at their heels relentlessly until we get them moving in the direction we envision. Only then can we can achieve the positive changes we seek and put an end to the present foulness of governmental systems.

Regardless of whether or not the Democrats have named their jackass or the Republicans their elephant, The Responsible Party's Australian Blue Heeler will be known as **PERCY**. Our mascot's name comes from the one word motto of The Responsible Party: Perseverance.

The Responsible Party will adopt the motto of the old Northwest Company of the fur trade era. Like our party, the Northwest Company had to compete with older, larger and better financed competitors. Eventually, they were able to overcome their competitors and dominate their market, just as we hope to do in the political arena, by practicing their motto: perseverance. In order to attain success and accomplish the goals we seek, a great deal of perseverance will be required of both the leaders and members of The Responsible Party.

Our party membership pin will be a small triangular mirror (made of either mirror, polished metal, or some other reflective substance) that will reflect the image of anyone looking into it. Etched or printed along the lower edge of this reflective device will be the words – **"I am Responsible."** The three sides or points of the triangle will symbolize the Responsible Party's status as ***the third party.*** Additionally, the triangle is symbolic of the *fulcrum,* part of the simple tool referred to as the fulcrum and lever. A *fulcrum* can be moved to increase pressure on the object one is trying to move. T*he fulcrum point is also referred to as the balance point.* The central ideas of our new party are to increase pressure on the two major parties while also bringing balance to the political process.

This party membership pin will serve as a useful conversation starter when anyone looks at the pin and sees his or her own image looking back. The message at the bottom of the pin will not only signal that the wearer is a member of The Responsible Party, it will also point out who is ultimately responsible for all personal decisions and their consequences, whether positive or negative, in our free society.

Our mascot, the Australian Blue Heeler, Percy, will stand atop our party pin.

Our Responsible Party membership cards will feature Percy, our motto, and our triangular mirror with its message of responsibility. They will be made of plastic and look similar to a credit card. Party member names and membership numbers (assigned in chronological order as members join) will also be displayed on the card. (I claim card number one!)

XI. The Future

The future of The Responsible Party belongs to those citizens who have had enough of governmental systems as they operate today.

Will those of us who are not happy with our governmental systems just continue to complain? Will we continue to proclaim the self-fulfilling prophecy that there really is nothing we can do to change the way our government systems are operated and perpetuated? Worse yet, will we simply chuckle ruefully about the political quagmire and wink at continued corruption, bribery and slipshod governmental management practices? Will we allow political favoritism, bribery, and influence peddling to simply continue unabated or become even more flagrant? Will we just give up when members of the major political parties claim that we have the best government there is and assure us that we can do no better?

I sincerely hope not!

It would seem the following questions need to be answered:

1.) **Can** The Responsible Party become a reality?

2.) **Should** The Responsible Party become a reality?

3.) **Will** a political party which gives a voice to middle-class Americans (neither the very rich nor the very poor) affect positive change on the American political landscape?

4.) Can and will a political party interested in neither the radical left nor the radical right be effective as a political force in the United States of America? In other words, is moderation and common sense a virtue?

5.) Are sound reasoning, practicality and results-oriented political analysis worthy goals in light of the radical emotionalism which drives the present political system?

6.) Will Americans respond favorably to a political party that takes the high road on the campaign trail?

The questions above are meaningless unless concerned citizens have the strength of will to make this new political option, The Responsible Party, available to the voting public.

So, of all the questions — Should we? Can we? Will we? — the biggest question is undoubtedly **WILL WE?** We know we should and can form this new political party, but **WILL WE?**

We Will!

There is much work to do. Let us begin!

XII. Think about this...

Picture the following:

Two railroad trains are traveling in the same direction down two sets of parallel tracks — one on the right and one on the left. The two sets of railroad tracks are very distant from one another and the vast expanse between them seems to be widening. The area between the tracks, though beautiful, remains uninhabited. The steel rails of the track upon which both trains are traveling are very worn, almost to the point of being worn out. The rail beds consist of rotted or broken ties and loose spikes and plates which have resulted in very dangerous conditions. While aware of the dangerous conditions of these tracks, management of both railroads have made the decision to disregard these issues because they feel they are of secondary importance to the uninterrupted movement of the trains and the convenience of the passengers and bags they carry.

A closer look reveals several interesting features about the trains and the tracks. Both locomotives are antiquated steam locomotives of the pre-Civil War era. These relics from the past lack the efficiency of more current technology, yet they continue on their course, slowly clanking and clunking along their dangerous pathway. No matter how much fuel they burn, these old engines are not capable of improving in efficiency or effectiveness. Increasing the quantity of fuel in the fire box only generates added heat and more soot, which flows out of the stack. Increasing the quantity of fuel burned is a complete and total waste of resources. The clanking and clunking continues at the same old pace.

Both antique locomotives are chugging along on a path they cannot change or alter. Locomotives, after all, cannot be steered but must follow along their set steel pathways. Any change in course can occur only when a switchman throws a switch. But the old switchmen of the past are gone, and the switching mechanisms are rusted and inoperable from disuse, so these old engines are destined to chug along on the same old worn out tracks.

An overview of the scene reveals yet other things of interest. To the left of the left hand track and to the right of the right hand track, a curious assortment of smaller vehicles is moving. These oddly diverse vehicles seems to be headed more or less in the same direction as the trains, but many seem lost or confused as they veer and swerve along their individual paths. Some are as old as antique bicycles, while others are as modern as scooters. Apart from traveling on either the far right or far left of the two trains, their passengers have little in common and very little chance of communicating with each other or with the passengers on the trains. Because these vehicles are much smaller, they also carry far fewer passengers.

All passengers boarding the old trains do so with the understanding that they are climbing aboard a train which is on a fixed and predetermined path. There can be no change of course because the rails only head in one direction, and there are no switchmen left to operate the old and rusting switching mechanisms. All the passengers are soon covered with the soot and grime produced by the old steam engines, and as more fuel is wastefully added, the contamination only gets worse and the passengers only get dirtier.

Since there is no possibility of a change in course, the only prospect for the future is that the worn out, dangerous old track system will eventually cause a derailment. Will management blindly continue to avoid making the necessary repairs to the tracks until such a catastrophe occurs?

Probably!

Now envision, entering into that ever-widening, un-inhabited openness between the two old rail systems, a state-of-the-art personal passenger jet aircraft. The aircraft is not shackled by the forces of gravity, nor is it on a predetermined path. The aircraft, though small in size, is extremely nimble and offers passengers an exhilarating ride. Passengers enter the aircraft clean and leave just as clean.

Because it is not bound by old worn out systems and predetermined paths, the nimble aircraft can soar, dive, veer right or veer left as need be. If the passengers on board the plane see something of interest on the old trains, the aircraft can get close to either of them, and the passengers can do this without getting covered in soot and grime like the train passengers. The jet can distance itself from either or both of the old trains if it should so choose. This is truly a fun ride.

The aircraft liberates its passengers from the entrapments of old, worn out systems and dilapidated, predetermined pathways. Passengers feel true freedom at last.

Which of these rides is of the most interest to you?

Contact us at:
www. Responsibleparty.org